MOUNTAIN GR

MOUNTAIN CREATURES

Sujatha Menon

PowerKiDS
press.

New York

Published in 2008 by The Rosen Publishing Group, Inc.
29 East 21st Street, New York, NY 10010

Copyright © 2008 Really Useful Map Company (HK) Ltd.

First Published: 2006
Designed by Q2A Media

Picture credits:
t: Top, b:Bottom, m: Middle, l: Left, r: Right c: Center

6t: R, 6b: Eyecrave, 7t: Casanova, 7b: Welland Lau, 8t: Jan Daly, 9b: Joshua Haviv,
10br: Impalastock, 12t: Joshua Haviv, 12b: Razvan Stroie, 13t: Friday | Dreamstime.com,
14t: Ulrike Hammerich, 14b: Galina Dreyzina, 15t: Richard C. Bennett, 16: Tamir Niv,
17t: Chinatiger, 17b: Steve Fine, 18t: Susan Kehoe, 18b: Sl, 19t: Pomortzeff,
20t: LeonD, 20b: Jadson, 21t: WizData, Inc., 21b: Joshua Haviv, 22t: Jennifer Nickert, 22b: Mshake,
23bl: Michael Shake, 24: Wesley Aston, 25t: Wesley Aston, 25b: Andrew F. Kazmierski,
26t: Carolyne Pehora, 26b: Travelshots, 27t: Wendy M. Simmons, 27b: Chee-Onn Leong,
28t: Global_Exposure, 29b: Zastavkin, 30b: Timberlakephoto, 31b: Clayc3466,
32t: Robert Fullerton, 32b: Tulissidesign, 33t: Amma, 33b: Courtnee Mulroy,
34t: Odelia | Dreamstime.com, 34-35c: Odelia Cohen, 34b: Xixau | Dreamstime.com ,
35t: Sathish V J, 36: Josue Adib Cervantes Garcia, 37t: Kevin Lepp,
36-37b: Josue Adib Cervantes Garcia, 38b: Nathalie Speliers Ufermann ,
39t: Kiryay | Dreamstime.com, 39b: Glen Gaffney, 40t: Chad King,
41: Phil Bull, 42b: PhotoCreate, 43b: WizData, inc.,

Library of Congress Cataloging-in-Publication Data

Menon, Sujatha.
  Mountain creatures / Sujatha Menon.
    p. cm. — (Wild creatures)
  Includes index.
  ISBN-13: 978-1-4042-3877-0 (library binding)
  ISBN-10: 1-4042-3877-8 (library binding)
  1. Mountain animals—Juvenile literature. I. Title.
  QL113.M46 2008
  591.753—dc22

2007008670

Manufactured in China

CONTENTS

LIFE ON THE MOUNTAINS

Mountains make up about a fifth of the Earth. They give us about 80 percent of the world's fresh water and support an amazing number of animals, birds and plants.

Too cold to bear!

It can be extremely cold up in the mountains. Even in summers, temperatures do not rise above 59° F (15° C) in many mountain regions. In winters, for as long as six to eight months, temperatures can fall below freezing. Since the air is so thin, plants and trees do not grow beyond a certain point. However, some animals and birds are capable of living even above the treeline. These creatures have developed special characteristics to fight the harsh conditions.

Life on the mountains is not easy because of the harsh climate, strong winds, snowstorms and slippery ice.

Woolly protection

Most mountain animals have a thick, furry coat that keeps them warm through winter. For some, this coat is thinner in summer. Even the feet are protected by fur. Some mountain creatures also have small ears and short legs that reduce heat loss. They are usually warm-blooded, although certain insects are also found here. However, reptiles cannot survive the harsh weather, because they would freeze.

Bighorn sheep have a thick coat to protect them in freezing temperatures.

Walking on ice

It is not easy to walk on snow or ice. If the snow is deep, feet sink in, and one can slip and fall on ice. So how do mountain creatures get around in winter? Most animals that live on mountains have a leathery pad on the bottom of their feet. This pad helps them get a good grip on the ice. The paws of animals like the snow leopard and cougar are large. This distributes their weight and prevents them from sinking into the snow.

These are the paws of a snow leopard.

Other adaptations

The higher one climbs a mountain, the more difficult it is to breathe. This is because there is very little air at high altitudes. How do mountain creatures breathe in such conditions? All mountain creatures have large and powerful lungs, and more hemoglobin in their blood. These special features help the mountain animals to breathe easily even at high altitudes. Some sleep through the winter. Bears are known to sleep all through the winter in caves or under the ground. Animals that hibernate eat a lot just before winter. They then retreat into warm burrows or caves and sleep until spring. Some animals, especially birds, migrate to warmer regions for the winter.

The pika is one of the mountain creatures that does not hibernate and is active throughout the freezing winter.

COUGAR

The cougar is also known as a puma, catamount and mountain lion. It is found in North, Central and South America. It is the largest wild cat in North America after the jaguar.

Cougar watch

Cougars live in rainforests, prairies, deserts and mountains. Depending on their habitat, cougars have a sandy brown to reddish brown coat. Cougars that live on mountains have a thicker coat. The fur is short and has no markings. The cougar has a small head, short, rounded ears and muscular legs. The hind legs are longer than the front legs.

Skilled hunter

Cougars are excellent hunters. They stalk their prey for a while, and then pounce on it. A cougar can leap about 40 feet (12 m), and jump vertically about 16 feet (5 m). Once the cougar has caught its prey, it kills the victim by biting its neck, using sharp teeth. After eating, cougars bury the remains of their prey, saving it for another meal.

This is the mighty cougar.

🐾 Here is a mother cougar teaching her cub to hunt a red deer.

Young cougars

A female cougar gives birth to 2 to 4 cubs. Cougar cubs are born with spots that disappear completely by 15 months. They remain with their mother for about two years. When they are old enough, the cubs leave their mother to mark their own territory. The cubs of a litter usually stay together until they are confident enough to settle in their own home ranges.

Living alone

Cougars prefer to live alone and are protective about their territory. A male cougar's home range rarely overlaps that of another male. However, males can share small parts of their home range with females. Territories are marked with scratches on logs, claw marks on the dirt or snow and with urine.

CREATURE PROFILE

Common name:	Cougar
Scientific name:	*Felis concolor*
Found in:	North, Central and South America
Size:	Adult males: 150-230 pounds (68-104 kg)
	Adult females: 77-132 pounds (35-60 kg)
Prey:	Deer, elk, beavers, porcupines, raccoons and squirrels
Enemies:	Humans. Cougars are often killed out of fear or to protect cattle.
Status:	Threatened. There are less than 50,000 cougars left.

🐾 This cougar is scratching on a log to mark its territory.

SNOW LEOPARD

The snow leopard can be found in the mountain ranges of central Asia. It is well-adapted to its cold habitat. It has thick, whitish-gray fur with spots, a long furry tail and huge, furry paws.

Life in the mountains

The snow leopard has many features that enable it to live comfortably in the mountains. The cat's unique color provides good camouflage on bare rocks as well as snow-covered slopes. The snow leopard also has large nostrils, wide chest and short forelimbs. Its woolly undercoat protects it from the cold. The bottoms of the paws are covered with fur to keep the snow leopard's feet warm and prevent them from sinking into the snow.

Not a leopard

The snow leopard is not a true leopard. This wild cat cannot roar like any of the big cats, including the leopard. The spots on the snow leopard's fur are also different from those of the leopard. In fact, the snow leopard has dark gray rosettes with spots inside, like the jaguar. Its head and face is covered with smaller black spots.

The snow leopard is a large cat adapted to moving about in snowy mountain ranges.

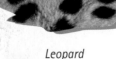

Snow leopard

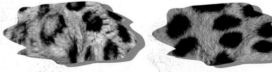

Leopard

Jaguar

The snow leopard has a long tail. It uses the tail to cover its nose and mouth in cold conditions.

Prey and hunting

Like all cats, the snow leopard is also a good, powerful hunter. It can capture prey more than double its size. It is known to eat any animal it can find, from large mammals like ibex and wild boars to small birds and rodents. The snow leopard usually stalks its prey and pounces on them from distances as far as 50 feet (15 m).

CREATURE PROFILE

Common name:	Snow leopard
Scientific name:	*Uncia uncia*
Found in:	The Himalayas, Altai and Hindu Kush mountains in central Asia
Length:	Adult males: 6–7 feet (1.8–2.1 m)
	Adult females: 5–5.5 feet (1.5–1.7 m)
Prey:	Ibex, wild boars, deer, hare, tahr, marmots and small birds
Enemies:	Humans. Snow leopards are hunted for their beautiful fur and also for their bones, which are used to make traditional medicines in Asia.
Status:	Endangered. There are only about 7,300 snow leopards left in the world.

Who's afraid of heights?

The snow leopard likes to lead a solitary life. This is probably why it lives high up in the mountains. During summers, the snow leopard climbs up to a height of about 19,685 feet (6,000 m)—even trees do not grow at these heights! In winters, however, this large cat comes down to the forests at an altitude of about 6,562 feet (2,000 m).

The eyes of snow leopards have round pupils unlike domestic and other small cats.

LYNX

The lynx is a medium-sized wild cat that is found mainly in mountainous regions. It has a short tail, a tuft of hair on the tip of the ears, and large, padded paws fit for a life on snow. It inhabits dense forests on mountains and rarely ventures above the tree line.

The thick fur of the lynx keeps it warm in the snowy mountains.

Three of a kind

There are three varieties of lynx in the world—the Eurasian, the Iberian and the Canadian. The Eurasian lynx is found throughout Europe and Siberia, while the Iberian lynx is limited to parts of Spain. Both species have thick, spotted fur, long whiskers and large feet. However, the Eurasian lynx is larger than its Iberian cousin. The Canadian lynx, found in Canada and Alaska, is closer in size to the Iberian Lynx.

The grayish brown coat of the lynx is occasionally marked with dark brown spots.

Hunting skills

The Iberian lynx prefers to hunt through the night, while the Eurasian lynx is active early in the morning or late afternoon. Both species feed on rabbits, deer, small birds and foxes. The lynx usually waits patiently for its prey to come close before pouncing on it. However, the lynx is also known to chase its prey over short distances.

CREATURE PROFILE

Common name:	Eurasian lynx, Iberian lynx. Canadian lynx
Scientific name:	*Lynx lynx, Lynx pardinus, Lynx canadensis*
Found in:	Europe and Siberia (Eurasian lynx), Spain (Iberian lynx), Canada and Alaska (Canadian Lynx)
Size:	Eurasian lynx: 40–44 pounds (18–21 kg)
	Iberian lynx: about 28–69 pounds (12.8–26.8 kg)
	Canadian lynx: 15–31 pounds (7–14 kg)
Feed on:	Rabbits, deer, hare, small birds, squirrels, foxes
Enemies:	Humans. All three species have been hunted for their thick, beautiful fur.
Status:	Iberian lynx—Endangered

The lynx has sharp pointed teeth for cutting and slicing the flesh of its prey. It has a bristly tongue that helps to scrape the meat off the bones.

Living the lynx way

Lynx lead solitary and secretive lives, coming together only during the breeding season. The lynx spends most of its time on the ground, although it can climb trees when necessary. The cat uses its extraordinary senses of hearing and sight to track down prey. Females take their cubs out on hunting trips to teach them how to hunt.

The lynx is solitary and elusive.

MOUNTAIN RODENTS

Rodents make up the largest group of mammals. Some common rodent species are rats, mice, squirrels, hamsters and guinea pigs. Most rodents live in forests and in the open plains. Some live in the mountains. They have special features that help them survive the very cold climate.

MARMOT

Marmots are large ground squirrels that live in North America and Europe. Marmots live in burrows and are social animals. A marmot colony can have 50 members. Sometimes, one member sits outside the burrow and keeps guard. When the guard spots danger, it warns the colony with a high-pitched whistle. Marmots are extremely territorial and defend their colony and young fiercely. Marmots mark territory by smearing rocks with a substance secreted from their chest glands.

🐾 *The marmot has a soft, thick fur, which keeps it warm.*

🐾 *The marmot lives in burrows and hibernates throughout the winter.*

ALPINE CHIPMUNK

Alpine chipmunks are found in the Sierra Nevada Mountains in California. They live at altitudes of 7,546 to 12,795 feet (2,300-3,900 m). Alpine chipmunks are the smallest in the chipmunk family. They are yellowish-gray and have light contrasting stripes. Alpine chipmunks mainly live on the ground, but can climb trees when in danger. Like all mountain rodents, alpine chipmunks also hibernate during winter. They eat a lot through summer, storing huge amounts of fat that come in handy during hibernation. Food is also stored away in burrows, so that the animals can eat whenever they wake up during winter.

The alpine chipmunk has stripes on its face, unlike ground squirrels.

CREATURE PROFILE

Common name:	Chinchilla
Scientific name:	*Chinchilla brevicaudata*
Found in:	Andes Mountains in South America
Weight:	1-1.5 pounds (453-680 g)
Feed on:	Grass, herbs and other mountain vegetation
Enemies:	Humans. Chinchillas have been hunted almost to extinction for their valuable fur.
Status:	Critically endangered

CHINCHILLA

Chinchillas are mountain rodents seen mostly at night. These furry animals are found on the Andes mountains in South America. Chinchilla are considered to have the softest fur in the world, which they are hunted for. The fur of these rodents is so dense that parasites like fleas cannot live among it, as they would suffocate. Chinchillas can often be seen bathing in volcanic ash, or dust to remove oil and moisture from their fur. They live in burrows or rock crevices and are agile, able to jump up to 5 feet (1.5 m) high.

The soft-coated chinchilla lives in burrows or crevices in rocks.

GIANT PANDA

The giant panda is well known for its unique black and white coloring. This member of the bear family lives in mountainous regions in south central China and is highly revered in the country. The panda is an omnivore, however, most of its diet consists of bamboo shoots and leaves.

Panda features

The giant panda has a bulky body like all bears. Its coat is mainly white with black legs, ears, shoulders and black patches around the eyes. The panda has an enlarged wrist bone that acts as a thumb and helps it grasp things like the bamboo. Pandas usually live on the ground but are excellent climbers. When in danger they can also swim.

 *The panda has a very thick, oily and woolly fur that keeps it warm in its cold and wet mountain habitat.*

Common name:	Giant Panda
Scientific name:	*Ailuropoda melanoleuca*
Found in:	Sichuan, Gansu and Shaanxi provinces of China
Size:	Adult males: 220 pounds (100 kg)
	Adult females: 176 pounds (80 kg)
Feed on:	Bamboo, mushrooms, grass, fish, insects, rodents
Enemies:	Snow leopards and eagles often seize panda cubs. Humans kill adult pandas for the pelt. The adult has no natural enemies.
Status:	Endangered. There are just about 1,590 giant pandas in the wild.

The panda eats sitting in an upright position, using its front paws to hold the food.

Living alone

Giant pandas are shy creatures and prefer to live alone. Males are not territorial and move in larger areas than females, who defend their turf. Pandas are active both during the day and at night. They are also very vocal and use different sounds to communicate.

Endangered pandas

Giant pandas are the most endangered bear species. Their main food source is bamboo. The destruction of bamboo forests has, therefore, caused a drastic fall in the panda population. Pandas were previously targeted by poachers for their luxurious fur. Wearing panda fur was once considered a sign of courage in China. Panda skin was also in demand in Hong Kong, Japan and many Asian countries.

The panda has five clawed fingers and an unusual wrist bone. The short claws help it to grab onto tree bark.

BLACK BEAR

Black bears are shy, so they live in places that are difficult to reach or have thick vegetation. These animals are usually found in steep mountains and thick forests.

This is an American black bear.

Bear facts

There are two kinds of black bears — the American and the Asiatic. Both species have a large, stocky body covered with shaggy, black or dark brown hair. They have small eyes, rounded ears, a long snout and a short tail. The Asiatic black bear has a cream v-shaped mark on the chest, and a small white crescent on the throat.

Good climbers

The black bear's hind legs are slightly longer than the front legs. The paws have sharp, nonretractable claws. The five claws on each paw help them climb, tear and dig. If ever you come face to face with a black bear, do not climb a tree, it will not help! Black bears are skillful and graceful climbers. They use their sharp claws to get a good grip on the tree trunk and climb quite fast. Black bears usually climb trees when faced with some threat. Mother bears send their cubs up a tree at the sign of potential danger.

The black bear is an exceptional tree climber.

The Asiatic black bear has a cream 'v' on its chest and has larger ears than its American cousin.

Sleeping through winters

Like most bear species, black bears hibernate. Animals hibernate to avoid the effects of winter. They eat voraciously just before the onset of winter so that they can store the necessary fat. Some black bears sleep right through the winter, while some sleep only during the coldest period. The hibernation period usually depends on the availability of food.

Waste to wealth

During hibernation, the bears do not excrete waste. Instead, they convert the waste material into valuable proteins. The heartbeat of the animal also drops during this time. However, the body temperature does not reduce much because of their highly insulating fur.

CREATURE PROFILE

Common name:	Asiatic black bear; American black bear
Scientific name:	*Ursus thibetanus; Ursus americanus*
Other name:	American black bears are also sometims called cinnamon bears.
Found in:	The Himalayas, Vietnam, China and Thailand; North America
Length:	Asiatic black bear: 4–6 feet (1.2–1.8 m) American black bear: 4–6.5 feet (1.2–2 m)
Feed on:	Grass, fruit, berries, roots, insects and carrion
Enemies:	Tigers, wolves and mountain lions feed on cubs and wounded black bears. Humans kill them for sport and meat.
Status:	Vulnerable

SNOW MONKEY

The snow monkey, also known as Japanese macaque, is the only monkey to be found in snowy regions. This species is found throughout Japan, especially in the north. It has grayish brown fur, red face and bottom, and a short tail.

Surviving the cold

The snow monkey lives in a variety of habitats, including places with freezing winters. It easily survives temperatures as low as 5° F (-15° C). This is because it has a thick, furry coat that grows thicker during winters. Snow monkeys also spend a lot of time in hot springs to keep themselves warm.

This female snow monkey basks in the sun.

Eating healthy

The snow monkey's diet changes with the seasons. It eats fruits and berries, seeds, leaves, roots, bird's eggs and insects. In summer, snow monkeys eat leaves and flowers, and in winters they feed on tree bark. The snow monkey is quite finicky. It always washes its food before eating.

A snow monkey uses its hands to eat.

Living in harmony

Snow monkeys are extremely social and enjoy playing and grooming one another. These peace-loving creatures help one another in caring and protecting the young.

🐾 *Snow monkeys keep themselves warm by hugging one another.*

A happy family

Snow monkeys live in troops consisting of 20 to 30 members. Sometimes the troop can have as many as 100 individuals. The size of the troop depends on the availability of food. These troops are made of a few adult males and more than double their number of females. The females normally spend their whole life in the same group, taking care of one another and the young ones. The males leave the group before reaching adulthood. They join and leave several groups in a lifetime.

🐾 *Every snow monkey has a unique face and soulful eyes.*

CREATURE PROFILE

Common name:	Snow monkey, Japanese macaque
Scientific name:	*Macaca fuscata*
Found in:	Mountains and highlands of Japan
Weight:	Adult male: 22–30 pounds (10–14 kg)
	Adult female: about 13 pounds (6 kg)
Feed on:	Seeds, roots, fruit, berries, leaves, insects and bark
Enemies:	Humans. Snow monkeys are considered pests and killed in great numbers by farmers. Deforestation has drastically reduced their natural habitat.
Status:	Threatened. The population of snow monkeys is declining drastically.

MOUNTAIN GORILLA

Mountain gorillas are found only in the Virunga volcanic mountains in central Africa. They are the largest of all primates.

Time for a nap! A gorilla is sleeping on soft grass.

Life in the mountains

Mountain gorillas have dark and silky coats, stocky bodies, long and muscular arms, large heads, and powerful jaws. Males are much larger than females and have sharp canine teeth. Adult males are called silverbacks as they develop a large patch of grayish silver hair on their backs when they mature. Their long hair helps mountain gorillas to combat the cold climate of the mountains.

Walk like a gorilla

Mountain gorillas have extremely long and muscular arms, and shorter legs. These creatures usually walk on all fours. They keep their feet flat on the ground, and use their powerful arms to swing the body forward. The weight of the whole body is supported by the knuckles that are placed on the ground in front of the animal.

The mountain gorilla's knuckles are specially adapted to take the weight of its whole body.

Common name:	Mountain gorilla
Scientific name:	*Gorilla gorilla beringei*
Found in:	Virunga volcanic range between Zaire, Rwanda and Uganda
Size:	Adult male: 450–500 pounds (204–227 kg)
	Adult female: 150–250 pounds (68–113 kg)
Feed on:	Roots, leaves, stems, shrubs, bamboo shoot, flowers, fruit, fungi and insects
Enemies:	Humans. Mountain gorilla habitats are being destroyed to make way for agricultural land.
Status:	Critically endangered. There are only about 400 mountain gorillas left in the wild.

All in the family

Like all apes, mountain gorillas are a highly social species. They live in groups consisting of one dominant male and a harem of females and their young. The young gorillas are taken care of by the females. Mountain gorillas are usually not territorial, but the leader can get aggressive if he feels threatened. The members of a group travel together.

Good communicators

Mountain gorillas communicate with one another using a variety of sounds. These include grunts, growls, chuckles and hoots. They also use facial expressions and gestures like beating their chest to communicate a wide range of emotions.

Grooming is an important part of a gorilla's social life. Female gorillas groom one another, the young ones and silverbacks.

RED DEER

The red deer, known as elk or wapiti in North America, is the second largest of all deer species in the world after the moose. This animal prefers mountains and open meadows and avoids dense forests. During summers, the red deer moves up to higher altitudes.

Fit for the mountains

Red deer range in color from dark brown during winter, to tan in summer. These animals have a characteristic light-colored bottom. Males have a shaggy mane that covers the neck. Red deer have heavy winter coats that are shed just before summer. They have a long head, large ears, short tail and long legs. Males have beautiful antlers branching out of the top of their heads.

Here is a small group of red deer.

CREATURE PROFILE

Common name:	Red deer
Scientific name:	*Cervus elaphus*
Found in:	Europe, and parts of Asia and North America
Height:	Adult male: about 5.2 feet (1.6 m) at the shoulder
	Adult female: 4.5 feet (1.4 m) at the shoulder
Feed on:	Grass, forbs and woody growth like cedar, wintergreen and red maple
Enemies:	Mountain lions, wolves, bears and humans
Status:	Excessive hunting for their skin and antlers has resulted in a drastic decline in the red deer population over the years.

Male red deer use their antlers to fight each other in the mating season.

Fighting for a mate

The red deer's mating ritual is called a rut. An adult male chooses a harem of females. Sometimes two or more males show interest in a harem, and they fight to decide the winner. Stags often bellow to scare the rival away. They also assess each other's body and antler size, with the smaller opponent often backing down. If neither stag backs down, it leads to a clash of the antlers.

Family life

A herd can consist of as many as 400 individuals. The male and female herds come together during the mating season and stay together through winter. In summer, the herds separate. The females leave to give birth. Females with calves often form separate nursery herds and take care of their calves.

Herds of male and female red deer come together in the spring to mate.

LLAMA AND ALPACA

Llamas and alpacas belong to the same family as camels. Both animals are found in South America and neither exists in the wild. Llamas were originally found in North America. They migrated to South America and became the main mode of transportation for the Incas.

The llama is an intelligent, friendly and obedient animal.

Unique features

Unlike a camel, a llama does not have a hump. Like camels, llamas have a long neck, rounded muzzle, a cleft in the upper lip and long, slender legs. The hoof pads are thick and leathery and help llamas get a grip on the rocky surface. Their long furry coats vary from white to reddish brown to black. They also have a lot of hemoglobin in their blood. This helps llamas survive at high altitudes, where there is little oxygen.

Beware, the llama!

Llamas prefer to live in herds of about 20. A male leads the herd and defends it fiercely. Males often fight for dominance, biting legs and wrapping their necks around one another. The male that is pushed to the ground is the loser. When threatened, llamas charge, spit, bite and kick the enemy. However, llamas are friendly creatures and make good pets.

The llama has bumps on the soles of its feet that give it a good contact with the ground.

Defending territory

Llamas are territorial even in captivity. However, if animals, like sheep, are kept in the same area, llamas adopt them and defend them. This makes llamas good guard animals for sheep, goats, horses and other domesticated animals.

ALPACA

Here is a llama and its young.

Alpacas look like large sheep with a long neck. Alpacas are smaller than llamas. They live in herds and are gentle and friendly. However, they can be aggressive when threatened. Alpacas have been domesticated for thousands of years. However, unlike llamas, alpacas are not used as beasts of burden. They are bred for wool and meat. The fleece of alpacas is luxurious. It yields much softer and lighter wool than the wool obtained from sheep.

The soft white fleece of the alpacas can be dyed in any color.

CREATURE PROFILE

Common name:	Llama
Scientific name:	*Lama glama*
Found in:	South America, near southeast Peru and western Bolivia and Chile
Height:	3.9 feet (1.2 m) at the shoulder
Weight:	300–450 pounds (136–204 kg)
Feed on:	Shrubs, grass, leaves, lichen
Enemies:	Mountain lions, cougars, dogs, humans
Status:	Domestication has helped to revive their population.

PIKA

The pika is a small animal that belongs to the rabbit and hare family. It is sometimes known as a rock rabbit or coney. There are about thirty different species of pikas, which look a lot like hamsters, even though they are more closely related to rabbits.

The pika has a stocky body, short legs and a small tail.

Life in the mountains

Pikas are found in cold climates. They are widely distributed throughout Asia, North America and parts of Eastern Europe. Pikas usually form huge colonies. Members of a colony gather food together and look after one another. However, some species prefer to lead a solitary life. In Europe and Asia, pikas have been known to share their burrows with snowfinches that nest with them.

Preparing for winter

Pikas are most active before winter. These creatures do not hibernate. Instead, they are active throughout. Some species spend the day basking in the sun, and crouching on rocks. Most pikas collect fresh grass and lay them out to dry. They then store this dry grass in their burrows. The dry grass serves as warm bedding as well as food for the animal during the harsh winter. Only the Royle's pika does not make grass piles.

The pika is a highly alert creature possessing excellent vision and hearing.

Family life

Pikas that live in colonies make burrows. These are very complicated and have many tunnels and entrances. This not only allows the pika to forage across a wider area, but also helps it to retreat quickly to safety in case of danger. Pikas find more food on the plateau meadowlands. Families are highly territorial, and males chase members of other families away, especially when they are busy drying grass and stacking hay.

 The pika bask in the sun on rocks matching the color of their coat.

CREATURE PROFILE

Common name:	Pika
Scientific name:	*Ochotonidae*
Found in:	Throughout Europe, and parts of Asia and North America
Length:	About 6–10 inches (15–25 cm)
Weight:	About 4.2 ounces (120 g)
Feed on:	Grass, twigs, flowers and sedges
Enemies:	Weasels, wolves, foxes, hawks and owls
Status:	Pikas are plentiful

ROCKY MOUNTAIN GOAT

The Rocky Mountain goat is a native of North America. Even though it resembles the common goat, the Rocky Mountain goat actually belongs to the antelope family. The main habitats of this species are the steep, rocky cliffs of alpine and sub-alpine areas.

🐾 *The Rocky Mountain goat is a very good climber.*

🐾 *The Rocky Mountain goat has large oval hooves with rubber-like soles that provide a good grip while climbing steep mountains.*

Physical features

Rocky Mountain goats have a stout body, which is covered with thick fur. The color of the fur varies from white to yellowish. Since they live in regions where it is cold for as long as nine months, they have a coat that is well adapted to surviving the freezing temperatures. They have a dense, woolly undercoat and long hair, about 8 inches (20 cm) in length, in the outer layer. This thick coat protects the goats from the cold and harsh mountain climate by keeping them cozy and warm. In summer, when the temperature rises, mountain goats rub themselves against trees or rocks to shed their woolly coats. Both male and female goats have prominent beards, short tails and long black horns.

Living in herds

Rocky Mountain goats form large herds during winter and spring. In summer, these animals form smaller groups or even live alone. Adult females lead a herd most of the time except during the breeding season. That is when males take over and participate in dominance fights to win over the females. Unlike other antelopes, mountain goats do not go in for head-to-head fights.

Warring nannies

Female Rocky Mountain goats, or nannies, also take part in dominance fights. For most of the year, a dominant female leads the herd. These creatures are protective and often become violent while defending their herd and territory. A fight between two nannies usually ends up involving the rest of the females in the herd too. Fights may sometimes lead to the death of one of the rivals. Weaker opponents usually give up by lying on the ground.

A nanny and her young one climbing a mountain. The calf learns to jump and climb when it is just a few minutes old!

CREATURE PROFILE

Common name:	Rocky Mountain goat
Scientific name:	*Oreamnos americanus*
Found in:	Parts of North America
Height:	31–39 inches (0.8 m–1 m)
Weight:	100–300 pounds (45.3–136 kg)
Feed on:	Grass, lichens, mosses, woody plants and other mountain vegetation
Enemies:	Mountain lions and humans. Golden eagles prey on the young.
Status:	Vulnerable. Mountain goats are killed extensively for their woolly coats and meat.

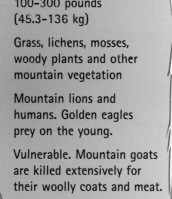

BIGHORN SHEEP

Bighorn sheep have been hunted so extensively that they are a threatened species.

Adult male bighorn sheep have such large, curved horns, no other name would have suited them! Females have shorter, less curved horns. The horns of the male and female bighorn sheep are adapted for their varying behavior.

By the age of 7 or 8, the bighorn ram can have a set of horns with a full curl and a spread of about 33 inches (83 cm).

Features of the bighorn

Bighorn sheep have a muscular body covered with smooth fur. The coat is similar to a deer's. The outer coat has glossy, brittle guard hairs over a short gray fleece. It is usually a glossy, rich brown in summer, but fades as winter nears. Bighorn sheep have a narrow and pointed muzzle, short, pointed ears and a very short tail. These animals have hard, double-layered skulls designed for combat. A broad tendon that links the skull to the spine helps the head to recoil from hard blows.

Locking horns

Male bighorn sheep are not territorial. However, they fight head-to-head for the attention of a female. Males charge at each other with their heads lowered. A male smashes into his opponent at about 20 miles per hour (32 km/h). The ram with the bigger horn holds an advantage. Fights often last as long as 25 hours, with five clashes per hour!

Built for the heights

Bighorn sheep can go up and down cliffs with ease. They usually use small ledges as footholds. Bighorn sheep can leap across distances of about 20 feet (6 m). Their hooves are hard outside and softer inside. This helps them climb easily at a speed of up to 15 miles per hour (24 km/h). On level ground, they can reach speeds of 30 miles per hour (48 km/h).

The bighorn sheep is a good climber and jumper.

Social animals

Bighorn sheep are found on the slopes of the Rocky Mountains in North America. They live in regions with light snowfall, since they cannot dig through deep snow for food. Bighorn sheep are excellent swimmers. They live in herds of 8 to 10 individuals but, sometimes, a herd can have up to 100 members. Males form bachelor herds. If a wolf threatens them, the herd huddles in a circle to face the enemy.

This bighorn ram is charging another.

CREATURE PROFILE

Common name:	Bighorn sheep
Scientific name:	*Ovis canadensis*
Found in:	North America, especially the Rocky Mountains
Weight:	Adult male: 264–286 pounds (120–130 kg)
	Adult female: 117–198 pounds (53–90 kg)
Feed on:	Grass and herbs
Enemies:	Mountain lion, coyote, wolf, bear, lynx and man
Status:	Threatened. Bighorn sheep populations have been falling due to poaching, diseases from livestock and habitat destruction.

IBEX AND TAHR

The ibex and tahr are types of mountain goats. The ibex is found in Eurasia and north Africa. Alpine ibex are usually found at altitudes of over 10,400 feet (3,000 m). The tahr is found in parts of Asia.

ALPINE IBEX

Alpine ibex have brownish gray coats that become dark brown during winters. Male ibex are usually twice the size of females, and can also be distinguished by their thick, prominent beards. Both males and females have long horns that curve backwards. In some males, the horns can be as long as 3.2 feet (1 m). The ibex uses its horns to fight off predators such as lynx, bears, wolves and foxes.

This is a male ibex.

HIMALAYAN TAHR

The Himalayan tahr is one of the three species of tahr. It is found in mountain slopes at altitudes of 11,482 to 16,404 feet (3,500-5,000 m). The Himalayan tahr is well-adapted to life in the mountains. Its hooves have a flexible, rubbery sole that allows the tahr to grip slippery rocks. The tahr is one of the best mountain climbers in the animal world.

The Himalayan tahr is adapted to life on the rugged mountain slopes of the Himalayas.

ARABIAN TAHR

The Arabian tahr is found in the Hajar mountains of the United Arab Emirates and Oman. It is the smallest of the three tahr species but very strong and extremely agile. It is capable of climbing nearly vertical cliffs. Unlike its cousins, this tahr is not found in large herds. It is also very territorial. This species is endangered because of hunting and habitat destruction.

A Nilgiri tahr has a hard-rimmed foot that helps it to climb mountains.

NILGIRI TAHR

The Nilgiri tahr is a goatlike animal with a short coat and short, curved horns. However, unlike the Himalayan tahr, the Nilgiri tahr is more closely related to sheep. Male Nilgiri tahrs are black with a silver saddle and short bristles. Females have grayish brown coats with white bellies. In all three tahr species, the males compete with each other for the attention of the females.

The ibex was once hunted extensively and is now threatened with extinction.

CREATURE PROFILE

Common name:	Himalayan tahr
Scientific name:	*Hemitragus jemlahicus*
Found in:	The Himalayan mountain range
Weight:	Adult male: 198–220 pounds (90–100 kg)
	Adult female: 132–154 pounds (60–70 kg)
Feed on:	Alpine herbs, shrubs and other mountain vegetation
Enemies:	Snow leopards and humans
Status:	Vulnerable. Overhunting and habitat loss has led to a sharp decline in the population of Himalayan tahrs.

ANDEAN CONDOR

The Andean condor is the largest flying land bird in the western hemisphere. It lives in the Andes mountains and belongs to the family of New World vultures that evolved from cranes and storks. Andean condors feed on dead animals.

Condor facts

Adult Andean condors are mainly black with a frill of white feathers at the base of the neck. When it flies to high altitudes, the condor tucks its head into this white down to keep the head warm. It also has a band of white feathers on its wings, which have a span of about 10 feet (3 m). The neck and head are almost bald. Male condors have a comb on their heads and a wattle near the neck. The skin of the head and neck can turn bright red to warn others. The feet have a long middle toe and the claws are straight and blunt, which helps them to walk.

Here is the large and majestic condor.

Condor in flight

The condor is a graceful bird. It can soar to great heights with minimal effort by using natural thermal air streams for elevation. Condors spend a great deal of time looking for food and fly miles to find something to eat.

Clean condors

Condors spend a lot of time grooming and sunning. Condors can be seen basking in the sun with their wings stretched out and turned towards the sun. They preen their feathers and arrange them neatly every day. They also clean their heads and necks after every meal. This is important as condors feed on dead animals, and the decaying flesh can infect them.

National symbol

The Andean condor is the national symbol of Colombia, Ecuador, Peru, Argentina and Chile.

The condor flies over a large area while looking for food.

Condor parents

Condors nest on rocky ledges at heights of 10,000 to 16,000 feet (3,000-5,000 m). The nest is made of a few sticks or twigs. The female condor lays one or two eggs at a time. The egg hatches in about 58 days. Both parents look after the nestling. The chick grows feathers after six or seven months. The young bird can fly only after it is six months old and stays with its parents for almost two years.

This condor is preparing to take flight.

CREATURE PROFILE

Common name:	Andean condor
Scientific name:	*Vultur gryphus*
Found in:	Andes Mountains in South America
Weight:	Adult male: 24-33 pounds (11-15 kg)
	Adult female: 16.5-24 pounds (7.5-11 kg)
Feed on:	Dead animals like rabbits, goats, cattle, deer, horses and coyotes, eggs
Enemies:	Humans
Status:	Hunting, habitat loss and chemical poisoning have reduced Andean condor populations.

GOLDEN EAGLE

The golden eagle is one of the most majestic birds of prey. It is found throughout Eurasia, North Africa and parts of North America. Most golden eagles inhabit mountainous regions, although they can also be seen in various other habitats.

Physical features

Golden eagles are dark brown, except for a golden patch near the crown, nape and sides of the neck and face. Males and females look similar. The birds have long, broad, brown-gray wings. The tail is gray-brown, while the head, body and smaller feathers on the front of the open wings are almost black. The sharp, curved claws are also black. The feet are yellow. To help retain warmth the legs are feathered down to the toes.

Bonded forever

Golden eagles mate for several years, or even for life. The mating pair chase, dive, circle and soar together. They also pretend to attack each other and lock their talons or claws in midflight. Nests are made of sticks, grass, leaves, moss, lichen and bark. Both parents incubate the eggs and care for the chicks.

The large, powerful feet of the golden eagle are equipped with fearsome talons that enable it to capture, kill and rip apart its prey.

Golden eagle facts

Golden eagles usually stay in one place. Some only migrate short distances for food. Most golden eagles are found either in pairs or alone. Young golden eagles sometimes form small groups. Adults form groups only during harsh winters or when food is abundant. Golden eagles defend their breeding area with aggression.

🐾 The soaring golden eagle has a wing span of 6 to 7 feet (1.8-2.1 m).

🐾 The mighty golden eagle has dark eyes and excellent vision.

Hunting together

Golden eagles feed on small mammals like rabbits, hares, marmots and prairie dogs. They also eat smaller birds, reptiles and fish. Sometimes they kill young deer, coyotes, badgers, cranes and geese. Golden eagles often hunt in pairs. One chases the prey until it gets exhausted, then the other swoops down for the kill.

CREATURE PROFILE

Common name:	Golden eagle
Scientific name:	*Aquila chrysaetos*
Found in:	Europe, North Asia, Japan, North Africa and North America
Weight:	7.7-13 pounds (3.5-6 kg)
Length:	29.5-33 inches (75-84 cm)
Feed on:	Small mammals like rabbits, squirrels, fish, reptiles, and birds
Enemies:	Wolverines, bears, humans
Status:	Vulnerable. Until recently, farmers killed thousands, fearing that the eagles would attack their livestock.

OTHER MOUNTAIN BIRDS

The mountains are home to a large variety of birds, including snowfinches, tinamou and chough. Some birds can be found at astonishing altitudes.

TINAMOU

Tinamous are one of the most ancient birds around and include 47 different species. Found mainly in the Andes, they bear a close resemblance to quails, although they are actually related to emus and ostriches. Tinamous have small, rounded bodies, and are able to survive even the harshest winters. They feed on berries and insects and are quite secretive birds. They lay several shiny eggs. The young can run almost as soon as they hatch.

The tinamou is protectively covered in grayish brown feathers.

SNOWFINCH

The snowfinch is a type of sparrow found in the mountains of Europe and Asia. It is a large and stocky sparrow about 6-7.5 inches (16.5-19 cm) in length. Most of these birds are found at heights of above 11,483 feet (3,500 m). Snowfinches are adapted to life at such great heights. These birds are so tough that they do not come down to the lowlands even when it is very cold, although they are known to move to slightly lower altitudes in winter. Snowfinches usually make nests in the crevices of rocks, but are also known to take up residence in the burrows of pikas. Their bodies are pale brown on top with white underparts. Their wings have long, white panels that are prominent when the birds are flying. They primarily feed on seeds, insects and worms.

Here is a snowfinch in its cold, rocky habitat.

Chough

The chough resembles a crow because of its black plumage. It is found in the mountains of Europe and Asia. It mainly inhabits the highlands. However, in some places these birds live in inland quarries. The two main species of chough are the red-billed and the Alpine chough. The red-billed chough is set apart by its bright red beak. The Alpine chough, on the other hand has a yellow beak. Choughs live in groups. They feed on insects in summer and berries in winter. Choughs are very acrobatic and are known for their graceful flight.

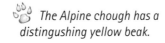 The Alpine chough has a distingushing yellow beak.

CREATURE PROFILE

Common name:	Andean tinamou
Scientific name:	*Nothoprocta pentlandii*
Found in:	Andean mountains in South America
Length:	9.8–11.8 inches (25–30 cm)
Weight:	1.7 pounds (800 g)
Feeds on:	Seeds, roots, fruit, small reptiles, insects and spiders
Enemies:	Humans. Tinamous are killed for their meat.
Status:	Eleven species are considered threatened, of which two are critically endangered.

MOUNTAINS IN DANGER!

Mountains are some of the most inaccessible places on Earth. Yet, despite this, human activities are changing mountain landscapes and endangering ecosystems. As a result, some mountain creatures, adapted to the environment and climate there, are dwindling fast. Global warming, deforestation and other unnatural events are affecting the life of mountain creatures, most of which cannot survive away from their natural habitat.

Global warming is melting glaciers.

Climatic changes

Global warming is one of the biggest threats to mountain ecosystems. An increase in overall temperatures has led to more glaciers melting. This means there is less snow cover. Creatures that live on mountains have thick coats that protect them from the cold. Warmer temperatures would make them uncomfortable and ill. Higher temperatures also mean shorter winters. Many mountain creatures sleep through winter. They eat more in summer. If winter days are fewer, these animals will feed longer. This can lead to a shortage of food.

Habitat destruction

Humans are also encroaching upon mountain regions. Forests are often cleared for agriculture. People have also started building more homes on mountains, cutting down trees. Many mountain animals depend on trees to give them protection from the weather and from predators. Deforestation also leads to a higher frequency of landslides and avalanches.

Large-scale deforestation means a shortage of food and habitat for many mountain creatures.

Hunting

Many mountain creatures are killed for money. Animals like the snow leopard, chinchillas and giant pandas are killed for their fur. Mountain antelopes are hunted for their coat as well as their antlers. Sometimes certain animals or birds are killed because they are considered pests. Condors and cougars were hunted as they were mistakenly thought to attack livestock. Hunting has brought many of these creatures close to extinction.

Herds of domestic cattle encroach on the habitat of mountain creatures and eat the mountain creatures' share of food.

Lack of food

Overhunting of one species often affects the animal that preys on it. Lack of food is one of the major threats facing mountain creatures. When people encroach on mountain regions, their livestock competes with the native animals for food. Many wild animals also catch diseases from animals like cats, dogs and other pets. Wild animals are extremely vulnerable to these diseases since they are not naturally immune to them.

Glossary

Abundant (uh-BUN-dent)
Plenty

Altitude (AL-tuh-tood)
Height

Antlers (ANT-lerz) A pair of long and branched hornlike growth on some animals.

Avalanche (A-vuh-lanch) A massive snow or ice slide

Brittle (BRIH-tul) Delicate and easily broken

Carrion (KER-ee-un) Dead or decaying flesh

Comb (KOHM) A growth, like a decoration, on the head of certain birds

Ecosystem (EE-koh-sis-tem)
Environment

Elusive (ee-LOO-siv)
Difficult to find

Extinction (ik-STINGK-shun)
To exist no more

Finicky (FIH-nih-kee)
Difficult to please

Fleece (FLEES) Thick covering of wool or fur on animals

Forage (FOR-ij) To search for food

Global warming (GLOH-bul WOR-ming) The heating up of the Earth's atmosphere

Grooming (GROOM-ing)
Cleaning an animal, often by brushing its fur

Harem (HER-um) A group of female partners for the male

Hemoglobin (HEE-muh-gloh-ben) The part of blood that carries oxygen

Hibernate (HY-ber-nayt) To sleep during winter to avoid the cold

Incas (ING-kuz) Group of ancient South American people

Mammal (MA-mul)
Warm-blooded animals, the females of which carry their babies inside their body

Migrate (MY-grayt) To move from one region to another. Birds and animals migrate for suitable climatic conditions

Nestling (NEST-ling) A bird too young to leave its nest

Glossary

New World (NOO WUR-uld) The Americas

Pelt (PELT) The skin or fur of an animal

Plumage (PLOO-mij) The covering of feathers on a bird

Prairie dog (PRER-ee DOG) A kind of small burrowing rodent

Predator (PREH-duh-ter) A creature that kills and eats its prey

Preen (PREEN) To smooth or clean with beak or tongue

Rosette (roh-ZET) Rings on the body of some animals like jaguars

Shaggy (SHA-gee) Long, rough hair

Solitary (SAH-luh-ter-ee) Living or being alone

Stalk (STOK) To follow prey

Stocky (STAH-kee) Well-built body

Taxidermy (TAK-suh-der-mee) The art of stuffing the skin of dead animals

Tendon (TEN-dun) A strong cord in the body connecting a muscle to a bone

Territorial (ter-uh-TOR-ee-ul) To defend one's own territory or area

Voraciously (vo-RAY-shus-lee) To consume a lot

Wattle (WAH-tul) A fleshy, wrinkled fold of skin hanging from the neckor throat of certain birds

Further Reading & Web Sites

Bredeson, Carmen. *Giant Pandas Up Close.* Berkeley Heights, NJ: Enslow Elementary, 2006.

Corrigan, Patricia. *Cougars.* Minocqua, WI: NorthWood Press, 2001.

Galko, Francine. *Mountain Animals.* Portsmouth, NH: Heinemann, 2002.

Kalman, Bobbie and Kristina Lublad. *Endangered Mountain Gorillas.* New York: Crabtree Publishing Company, 2004.

Simon, Seymour. *Gorillas.* New York: Harper Trophy, 2003.

Due to the changing nature of Internet links, PowerKids Press has developed an online list of Web sites related to the subject of this book. This site is updated regularly. Please use this link to access the list: www.powerkidslinks.com/wcre/mountain/

Index

Index